Under The Sea In The Bahamas
MusicArt Coloring Book

Velyn Cooper

ISBN-10: 1718950055

ISBN-13: 1718950054

COVER DESIGN: VELYN COOPER

VC Productions
vcproductions1@gmail.com

Under The Sea In The Bahamas
MusicArt Coloring Book

This book is a coloring and a teaching book designed to help children and any other interested persons, in identifying and learning a little about what is Under The Sea In The Bahamas. It also introduces basic Music Theory symbols such as staff, clefs, notes and rests, with their identifications listed at the back of the book.

The fun part is coloring the pictures and the exciting part is doing a little research and writing information about each picture, which then transforms the coloring book into a keepsake study and reference book that can become a part of an actual personal and literal paper book library.

Have fun as you discover some of what is Under The Sea In The Bahamas.

SOME UNDER THE SEA LIFE INTRODUCED IN THIS BOOK

Angelfish, Conch, Grouper, Hogfish, Grunt, Dolphin, Marlin, Turbot, Lobster, Eel, Crab

Angelfish

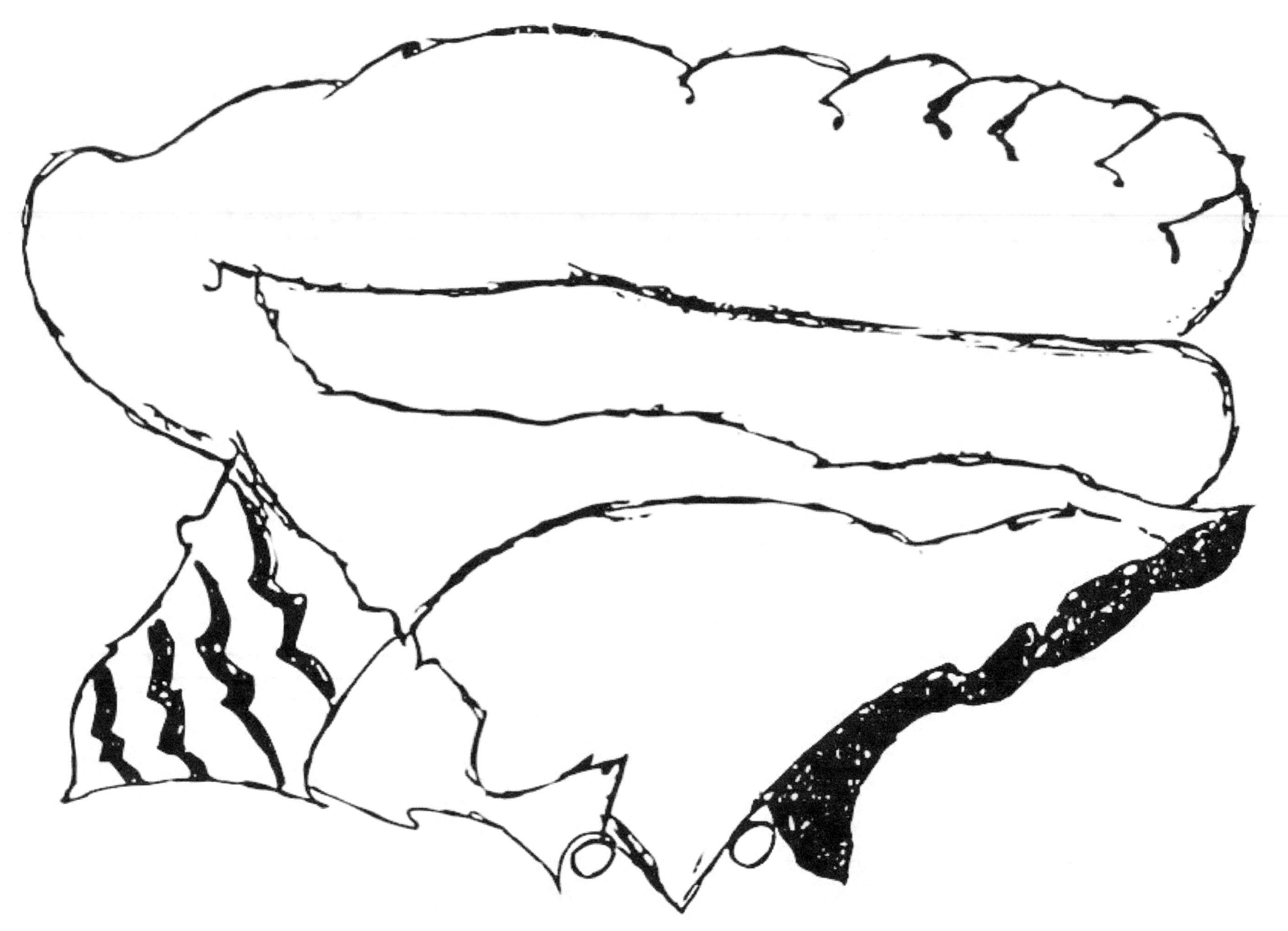

Conch

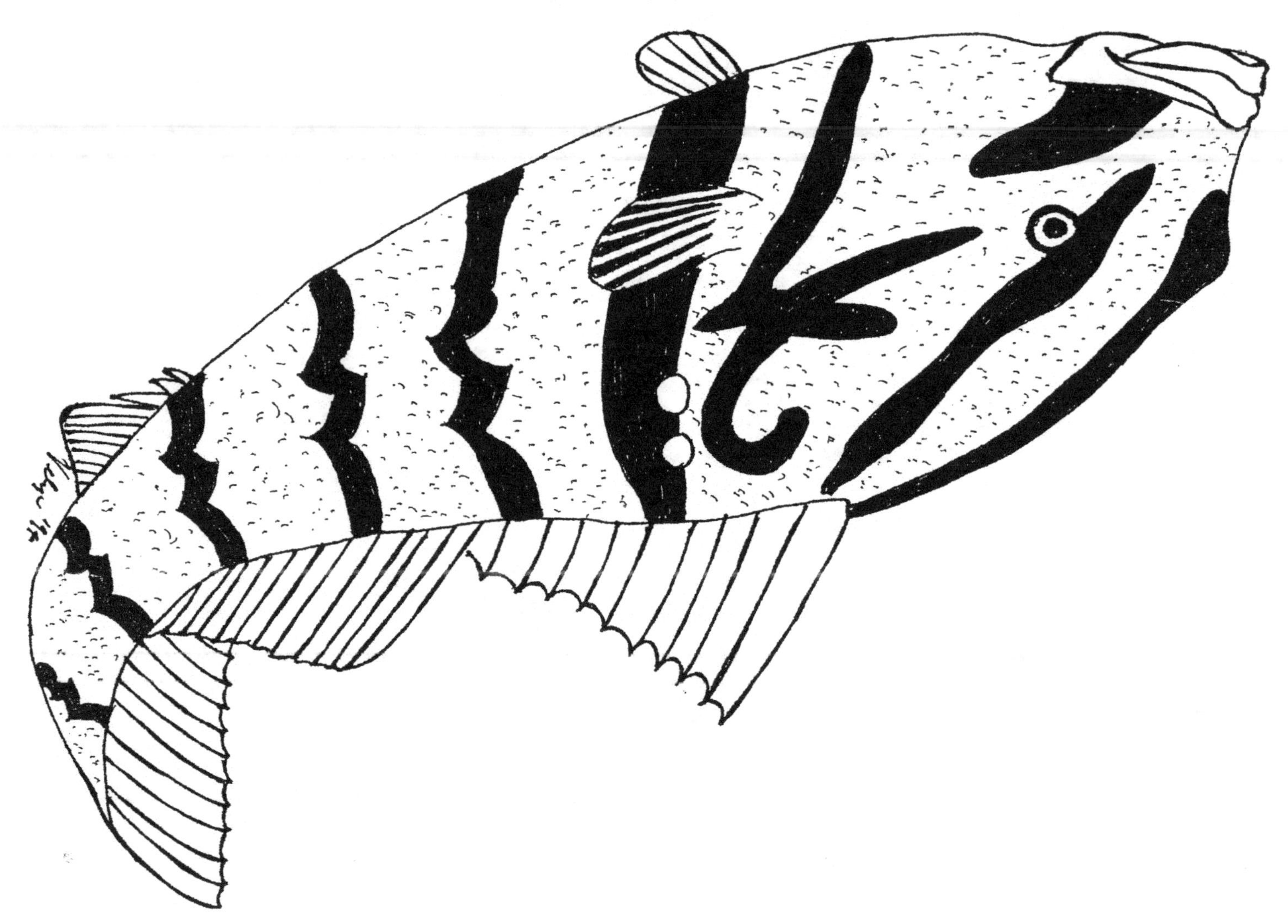

Grouper

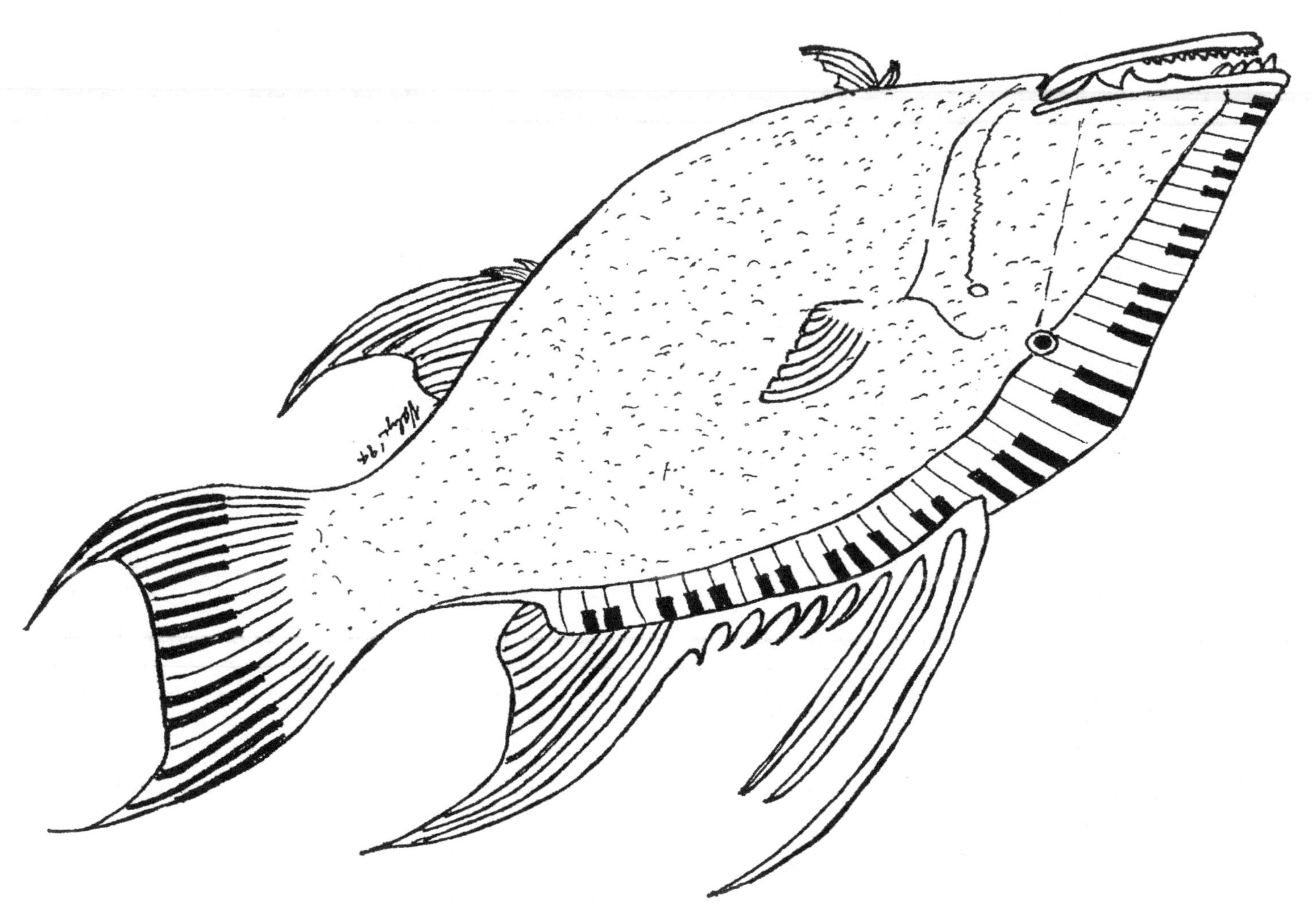

Hogfish

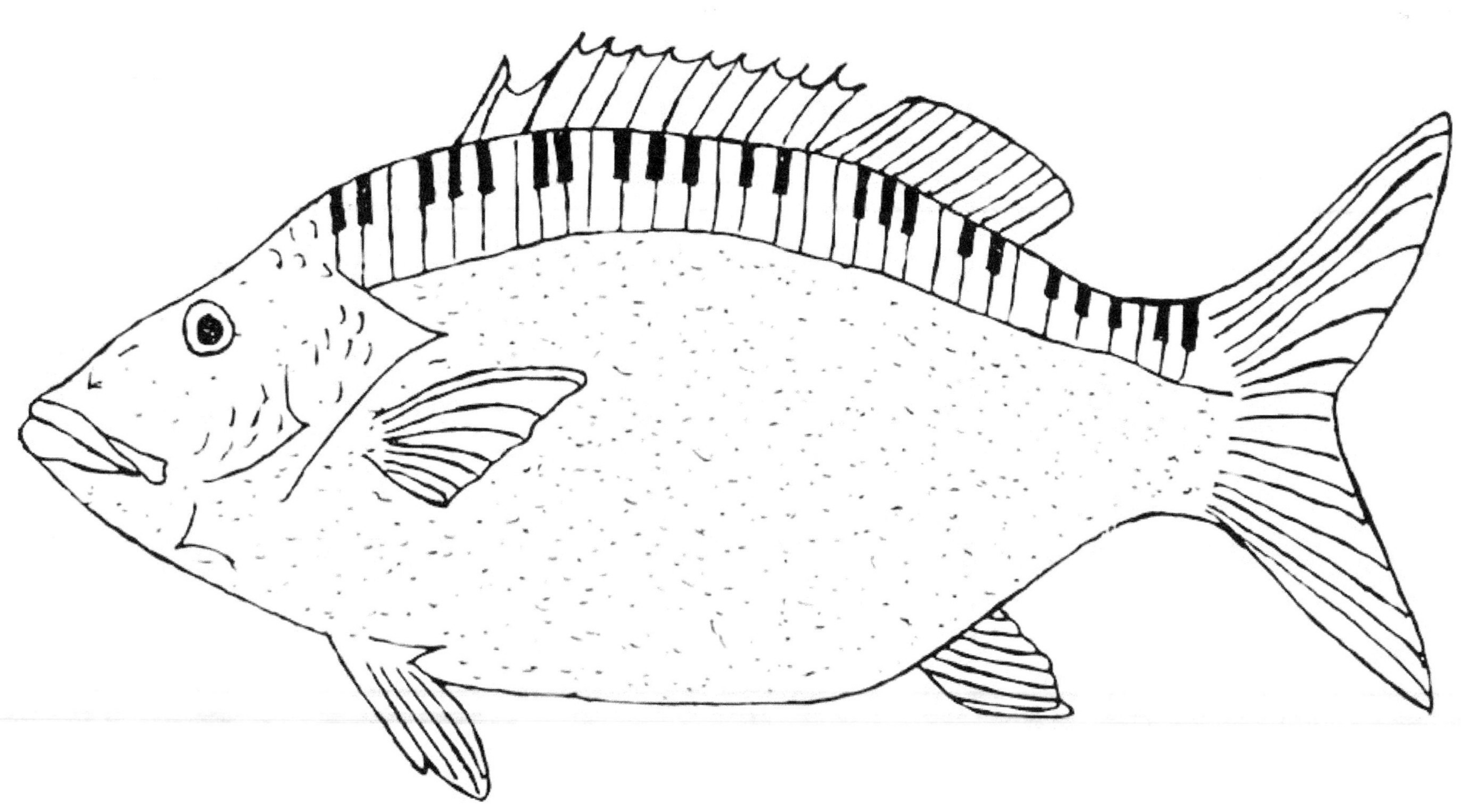

Grunt

Under The sea

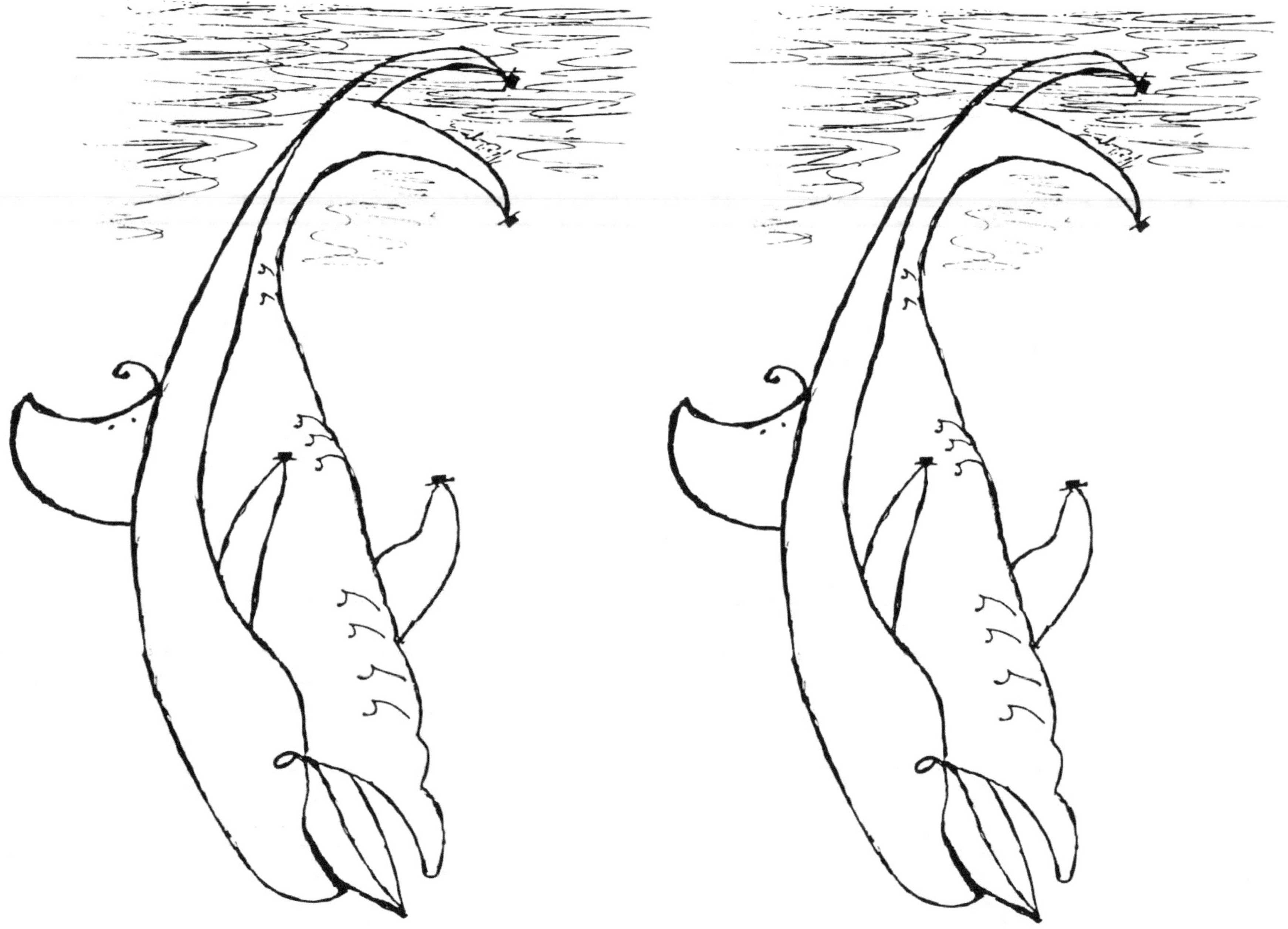

Dolphins

Marlin

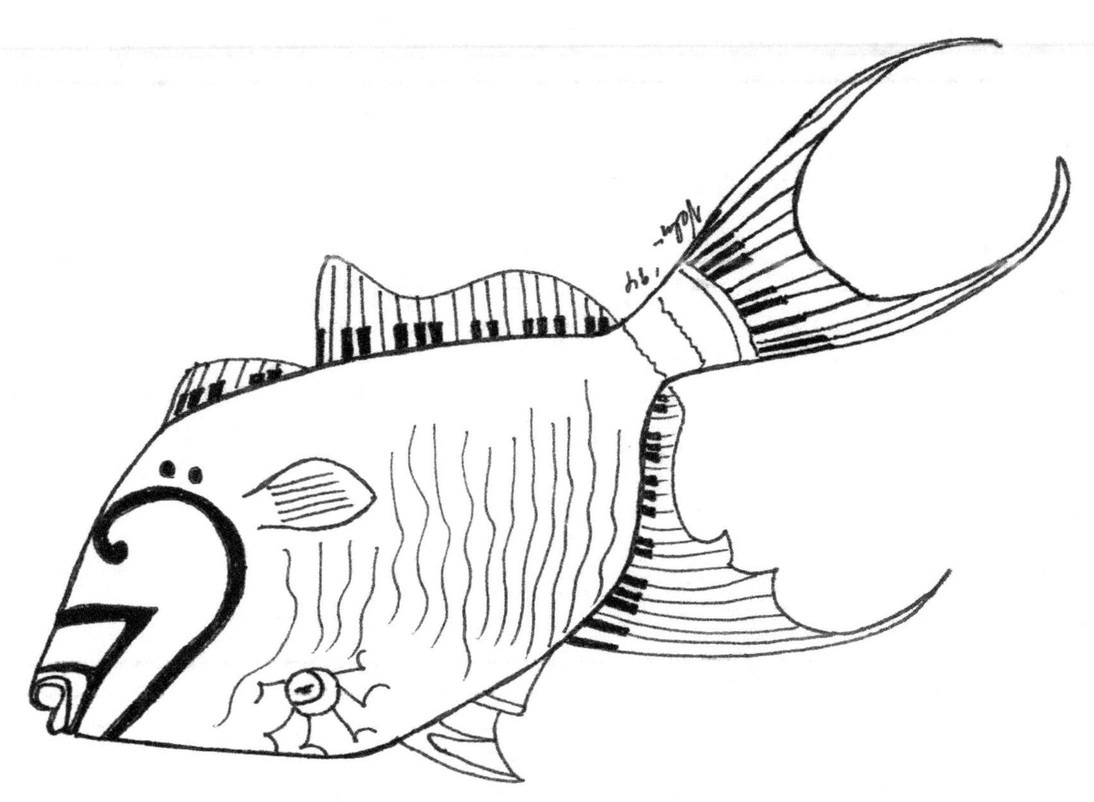

Turbot

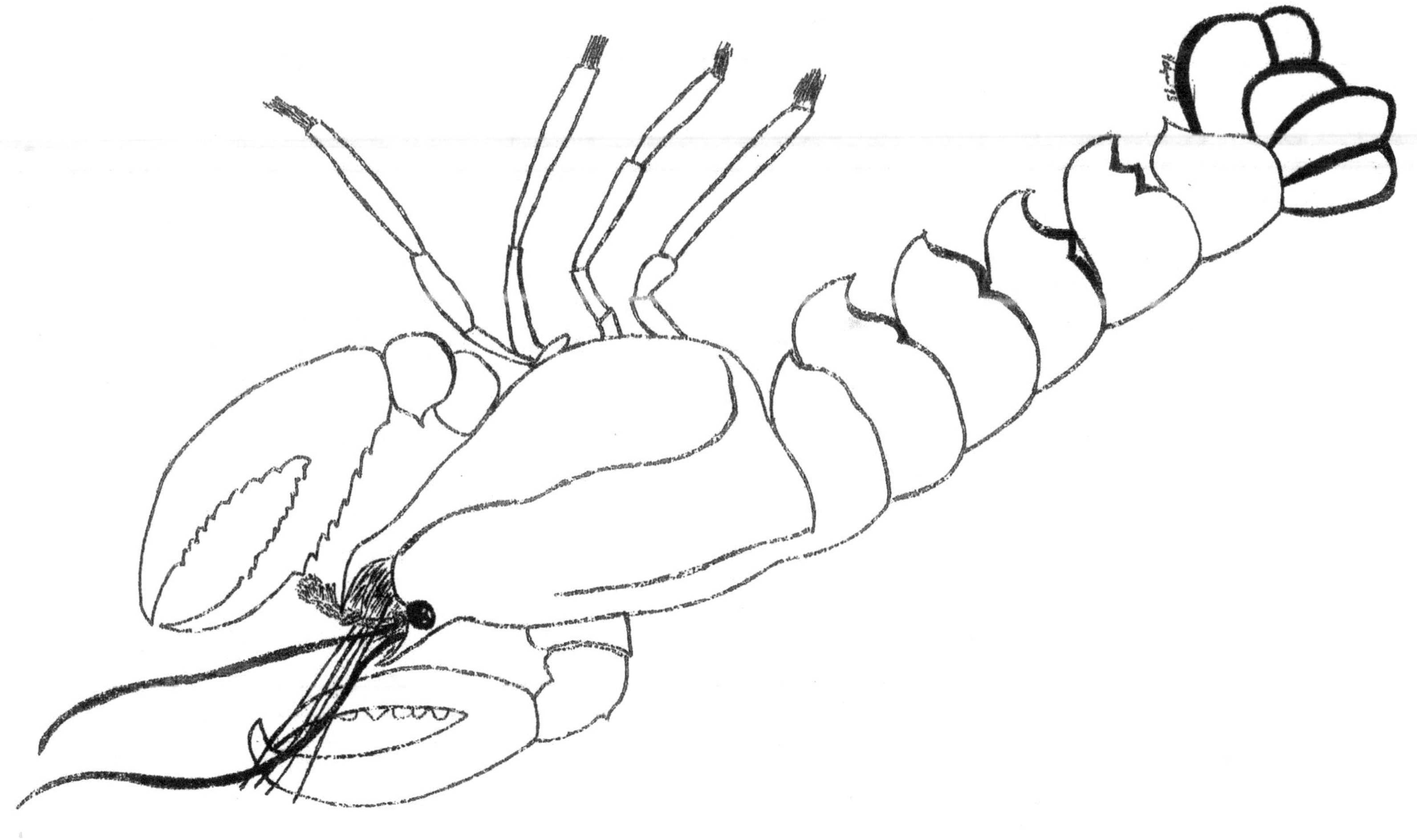

Lobster

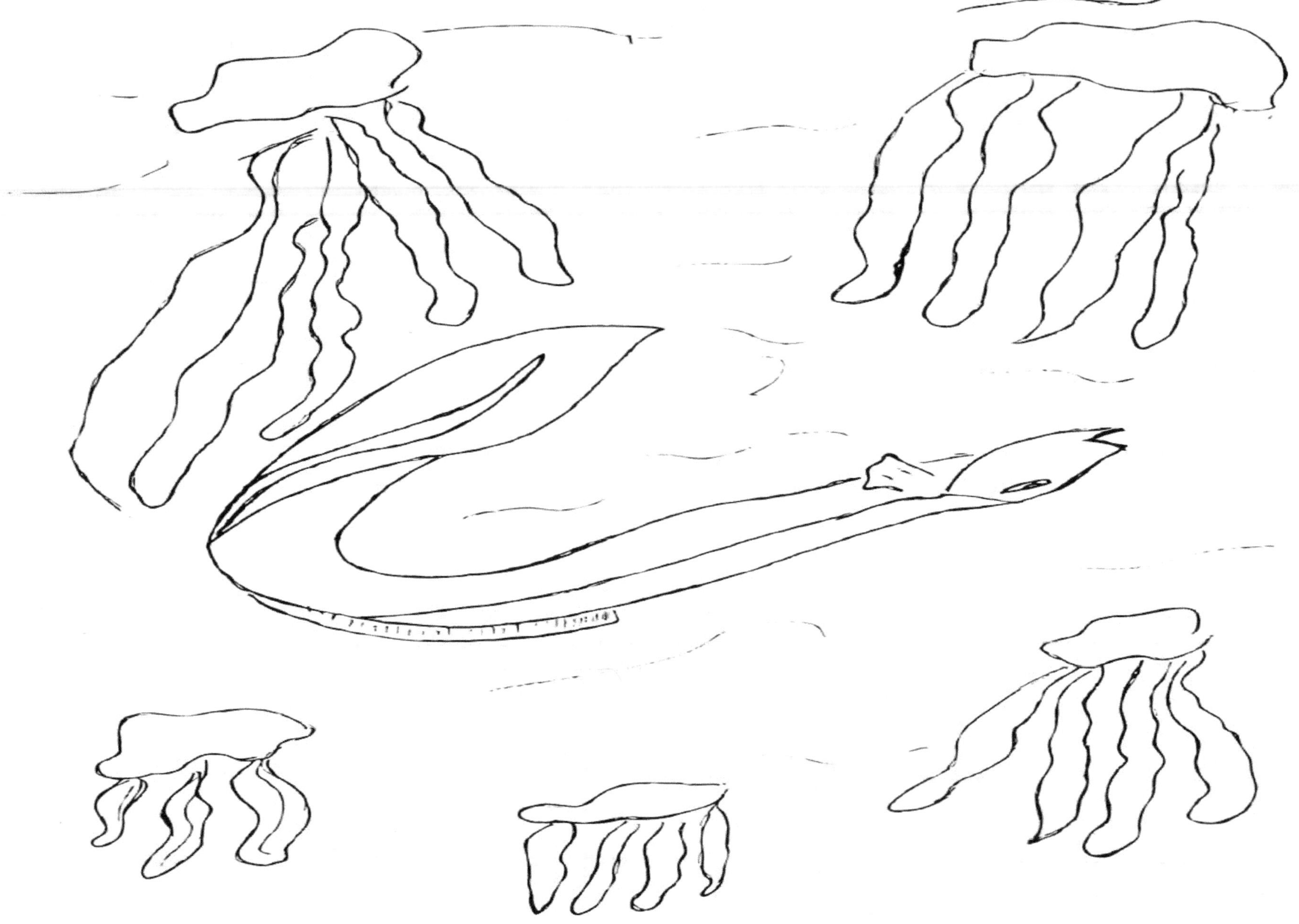

Eel

Crab

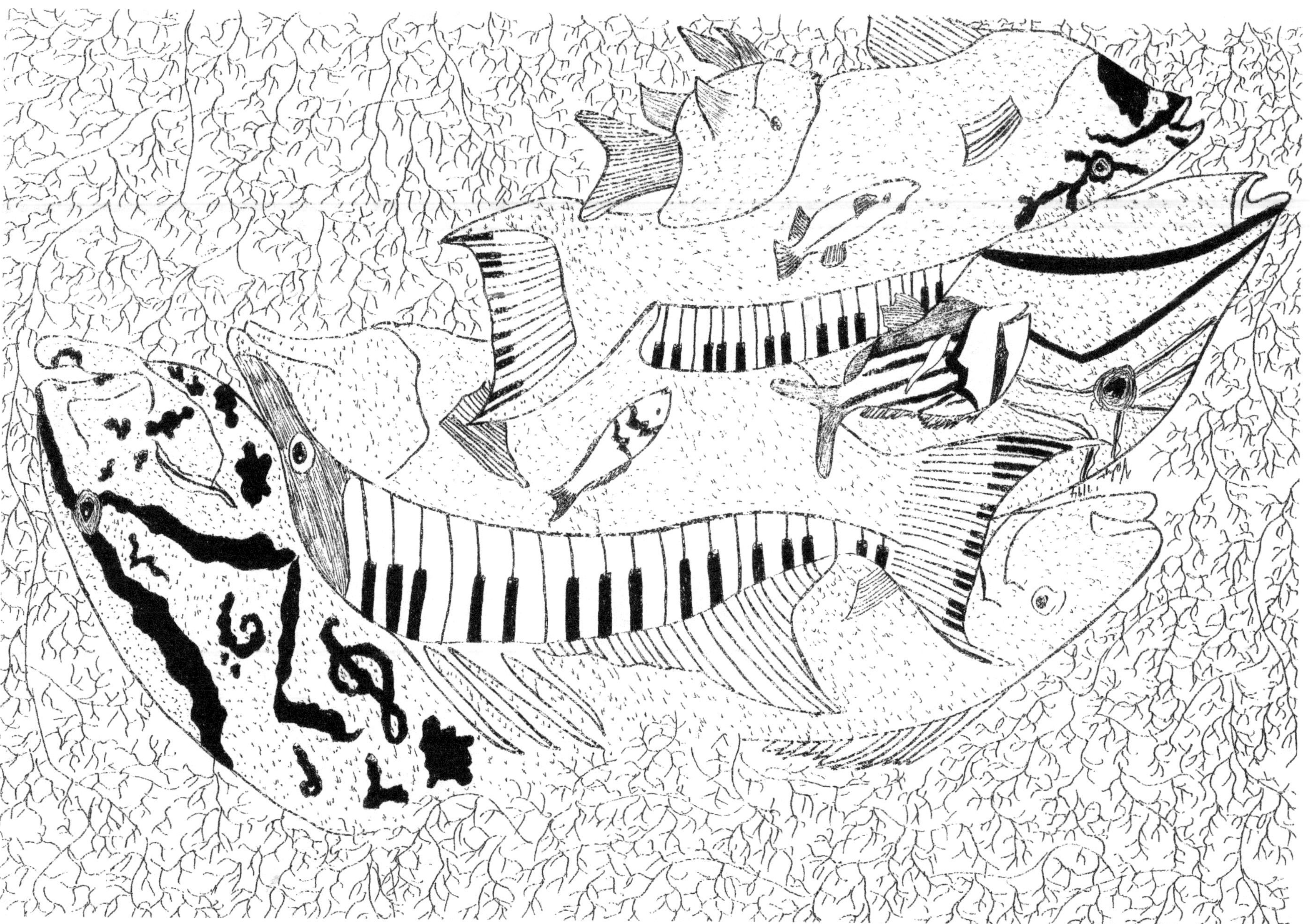

Under The Sea

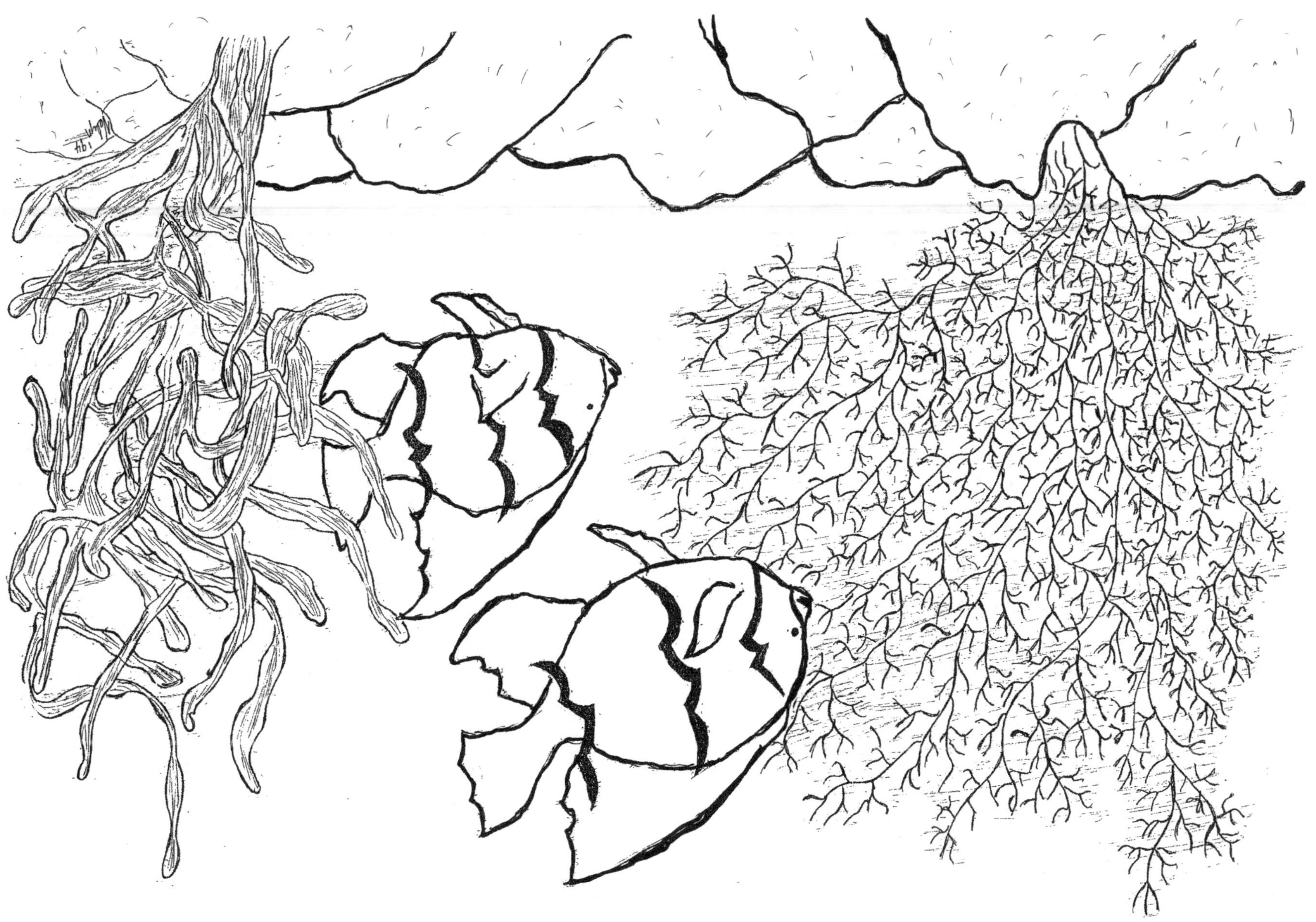

Under The Sea

Under The Sea

Under The Sea

Let's See If You Were Paying Attention.

There are two pictures in this book that have no music symbols on them. Which two pictures are they ?

1.____

2.____

Which music instrument is in the pictures?

____

Music Symbols introduced in this Book

Treble Clef   Staff   Bass Clef

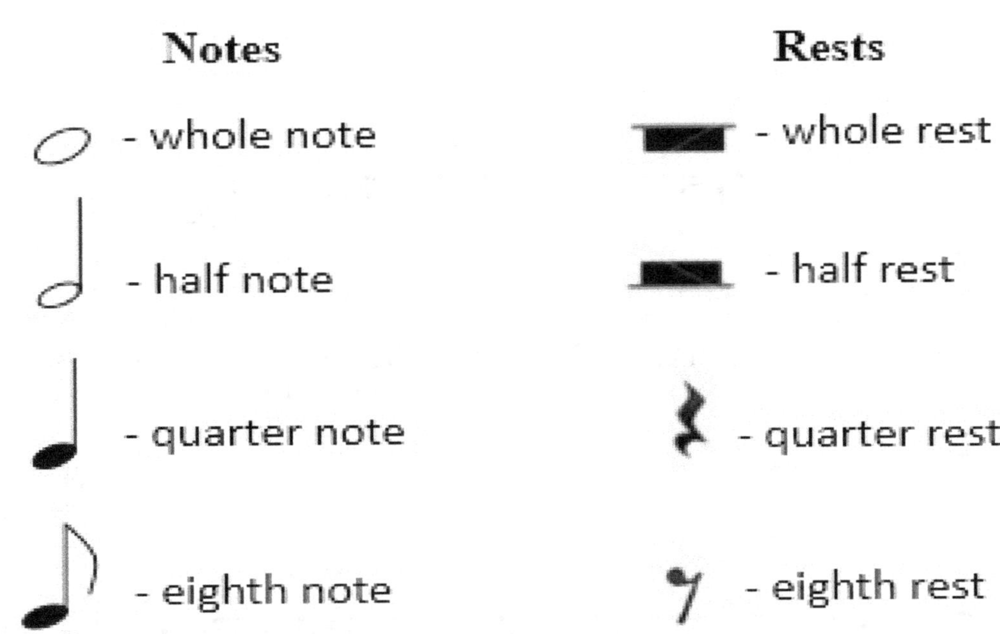

Other Children's Books by Velyn Cooper

Curly Tail
Curly Tail and The Sun
Four cats
One Duck/Two Ducks/Three Ducks
Rusty the Rat
Let's Have Fun with Music Series...Primer to Level 3
An Easy Approach to Learning and Understanding The Fundamentals of Music Theory
The Storyteller Coloring Books for Children

Other books by Velyn Cooper

Biblical Journeys: Passages Through Time and Into Eternity

Expressions of Love

Happy Mother's Day

High School Girls- Build A Strong Foundation & Face Your

Future Prepared & Courageous

High School Girls- Build A Strong Foundation & Face Your

Future Prepared & Courageous

Look to God in Faith

My Redeemer Lives – Photo Essay

Natural Arrangements – Unity in the Midst of Diversity

Poetry From the Heart

Reflections: A 90-Day Devotional

Renewing Your Mind — Transformation is a Lifelong Process

Shades of Pink – in Memory of Hartlyn Cooper Martin

The Beauty of Freeport, Grand Bahama, Bahamas

The Journey to Becoming a True Woman of Virtue

Thoughts: A Book of Quotes

Transitioning High School and Beyond —The Journey Begins

Understanding God Through Repentance, Confession and Baptism, Salvation

What Does The Bible Say About….

Perpetual Quarterly Calendars With Daily Inspirational Messages

The Storyteller coloring Books for Adults

If you would like to contact the author, please send your questions or comments to:

Velyn Cooper

P. O. Box F42524

Freeport, Grand Bahama

Bahamas

Email: **booksbyvelyn@gmail.com**

Website: biblicaljourneys.net

Be sure and check out our Kids Corner

http://www.biblicaljourneys.net/jabez-world-changers.html